WHICHFORD
& ASCOTT

O B S E R V E D

For JULIA

WHICHFORD
& ASCOTT
O B S E R V E D
The making of a Warwickshire village

JOHN MELVIN

"I know a bank whereon the wild thyme blows,
Where ox-lips and the nodding violet grows;
Quite over-canopied with lush woodbine,
With sweet musk roses, and with eglantine:"

WILLIAM SHAKESPEARE
A MIDSUMMER NIGHTS DREAM

W
WYSDOM PRESS

Acknowledgments

This study grew out of the work on the Village Plan. I'd like to thank all members of that committee for their thoughts and ideas which over two years have taught me so much about our small corner of Warwickshire. I hope that I have accurately reflected the feelings and views of the many residents who attended the various consultative meetings and workshops. The inevitable omissions and errors are entirely mine. I, as much as any of those on the Parish Plan Committee, owe an enormous debt of gratitude to Jim Keeling, whose patience and good humour does so much to sustain a sense of fun in our daily lives. I'd like to thank Trish Hedges for her work; her professional survey will remain a valuable tool whereby our two villages can be understood. I am grateful to Barry Hedges for his generous reading and commenting on the earlier draft of this book. I am indebted to Frances Lee who introduced me to many of the secret corners that abound in these two villages. Our neighbours and friends who, a few years back, welcomed my wife and me so warmly are too numerous to name, but I hope that this little publication can be taken as an expression of our thanks. Finally, I want to thank Julia, whose skills as an historian and editor literally made this book possible.

John Melvin
Ascott 2008

Cover: View of St Michael's Church from the castle.

First published in Great Britain in 2008 by
Wysdom Press
Whichford Hill House
Ascott
Shipston-on-Stour
CV36 5PP

ISBN 978-0-9533298-1-6

Distributed by Wysdom Press

Printed and bound in Italy

CONTENTS

PREFACE

This little book examines some of the more modest buildings of a simple Warwickshire village as well as looking at those buildings that are architecturally more significant. It tries to ask why collectively they make up our idea of a particular place. What is it that we can discover from these seemingly ordinary buildings that allows them to become something rich and aesthetically satisfying? Their very quality may in fact lie in this ordinariness; yet within this unassuming architecture may reside a valuable repository of skill and understanding.

All places change, and there is today a real desire to understand this change. To do this we must first recognise what makes the place special. What are those features that we should regard as permanent? What do we have to do to strengthen and retain them?

History should be our first guide, history will tell us who lived here and what were the institutions that helped to shape their lives. History does not lie just in deeds or documents; it is to be discovered by us all with our eyes, and even felt with our feet. A hedgerow or line of ancient oaks will tell us as much, and sometimes more than we can find on maps. The shadows that fall across a field from a four o'clock sun may reveal the presence of old strip farming or a disused quarry that helped to shape the settlement. Only by understanding the past will we correctly understand the present, and through this we can envisage the future. By first understanding a place we can imaginatively and emotionally possess it. If we possess it, we can love it and make it our home. As our home, our natural desire is to conserve and pass it on to the next generation.

Edmund Burke famously talked about that partnership between those who are living, those who are dead and those who are to be born. Just as we are heirs to the past, we have a duty to the next generation. Burke may have been writing as a politician, but his earlier *Essay on the Sublime and the Beautiful*[1] must have informed his vision of society. I believe profoundly that Burke's claim about the nature of the social contract has a particular relevance for us today.

The hope for this publication, which grew out of the village's work on a Parish Plan, is that it might be a bridge between those who live here and love the place, and those who have the responsibility to administer the complex and often cumbersome machinery of planning: the serious purpose of this book is to try and bring about a partnership of understanding.

View of Church, with thatched Barn of the Old House in the foreground.

LANDSCAPE SETTING

A little north of Chipping Norton, where the three counties of Oxfordshire, Gloucestershire and Warwickshire meet, on the farthest reach of the Cotswold escarpment can be found the two ancient settlements of Whichford and Ascott. From the west the approach to these two villages is through the parklands of Weston Park or up from Long Compton. The landscape here appears to stretch out before us as it were for our delight and possession. On a fine day it is even possible for the eye to catch a glimpse of the shimmering Malvern Hills. This is not the site of the ancient Forest of Arden, which lies twenty-five miles away, just north-west of Stratford-upon-Avon. Nevertheless it possesses many of the qualities of Shakespeare's Arden, which stood for an ideal sequestered pastoral retreat for lovers and for reflection. The name Arden is in fact derived from the British Celtic word 'Ardu' meaning 'high land', and this would appear to be the perfect description for the elevated causeway between Long Compton and Whichford.

Only the mournful figures of the Whispering Knights, that Neolithic monument at Little Rollright, disturb this idyll with a reminder of the transience of life. The power of these stones to disturb also has the power to console; deep within us we recognise that structures such as these, married to the landscape, can become poetic statements transcending time. In so doing we invest them with myth, and they become a reference in our daily lives, defining the landscape and even invoking a primeval sense of shelter. It is from these qualities that we form our idea of settlement and seek something of the sacred. This experience can never be too far from our thoughts when we consider Whichford and Ascott.

Whichford and Ascott are enclosed by the soft oolite limestone hills of Oxfordshire and Gloucestershire. The old drover's road from Bloxham leads to a deep descent from the high plateau. Our first glimpse of these settlements in summer is arrived at by burrowing down through a canopy of trees, which part to reveal these two villages. The hills unfold and seem to dance as they accompany our descent. An element of surprise on arrival is an essential ingredient to the experience, and this should be a key component, which any plan must recognise. So essential are these hills to our sense of place, that they must be held sacrosanct.

Public Fountain at the foot of Whichford Hill, one of several such structures to be found in the village.

HISTORICAL BACKGROUND

Whichford and Ascott are set in a dramatic landscape of extraordinary beauty that derives from a geological fault, formed in the Jurassic period.

This parish appears in the Domesday inventory as of some value in agricultural terms, but otherwise we know little of pre-Norman Whichford, except that one or two outlying roads are believed to have been Saxon drovers roads. The village of Whichford today reveals evidence of several periods of development: the Norman de Mohuns built the fortified castle and the Norman church; a pre-enclosures rural village of small strip farming contributed many yeoman farm houses to the village community; and finally, the presence of the enormous Weston Park Estate. Vernacular details from all these periods are to be found and valued.

The area around Whichford was at the centre of the Civil War, but today little remains of those turbulent times, save for the considerable damage done to the church by the Parliamentarians. The tradition associated with Traitor's Ford[2] tells the tale of one who betrayed Royalist troops to Cromwell's men, and reminds us of the hard choices that this English Revolution imposed on the people of these parts.

The population today c. 2007 is a little over three hundred, and is similar to that of two hundred years ago. Unlike many Cotswold villages, most of the population is still of working age, but unlike their counterparts two generations back, who were employed in agriculture, a growing number of the residents of today are able to work from home, linked to their source of employment by means of the new computer technologies. This trend is likely to grow in importance and should be allowed for in any plan.

Contemporary history is undoubtedly being made by the presence of the Whichford Pottery, whose reputation is worldwide and attracts many visitors. It has made a 21st century virtue out of the traditional craft of pot-making, which is linked so strongly with the history of the Midlands and its soil. The philosophy of life and work extended by this family of potters, the Keelings, has shaped modern Whichford.

The church gates, St. Michael's Church.

ARRIVAL AND EXPERIENCE

Whichford

The Green is the central focus to the village of Whichford. This large space is first defined by the magnificent chestnut trees, which in summer display their pink candles. Architecturally, the line of cottages and farmhouses terminating with the fine pair of semi-detached estate cottages on the eastern side [fig18] represents much of the best of the architectural character of the village. This group of buildings rewards close study; it demonstrates how incremental change can be accommodated over time. The Green is further contained by the charming former school building [fig 10], which makes the southern edge. On close inspection this building can be seen as a refacing of a simpler school building. The local stone is laid without mortar, resembling a dry stone wall. The over-large quoining around the windows may have been intended to convey a new sense of civic pride in the village school. On the north side The Norman Knight [fig11] occupies a pivotal site in the village, facing the Green, and extending a welcome to visitors. Its unpretentious façade of three bays lies behind the more recent pergola and pretty pub garden. The townscape quality of containment around The Norman Knight is not sustained because recent development has introduced conflicting scales that pay little regard to the street alignment.

Although the Green forms the immediate image of Whichford, its historic heart lies secretly in the area round the church and beyond [fig 9], as far as the remains of a moated Norman castle. This castle once commanded the valley, which today presents a willow pattern of pools, bridges and islands.

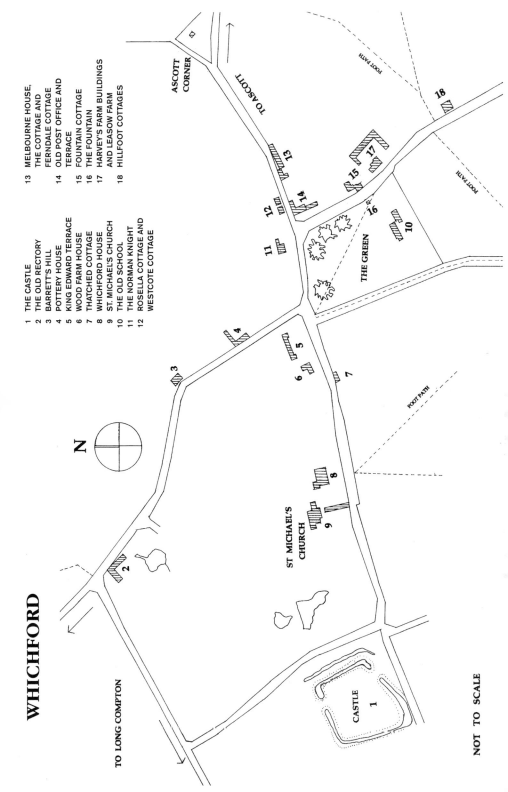

WHICHFORD

1 THE CASTLE
2 THE OLD RECTORY
3 BARRETT'S HILL
4 POTTERY HOUSE
5 KING EDWARD TERRACE
6 WOOD FARM HOUSE
7 THATCHED COTTAGE
8 WHICHFORD HOUSE
9 ST. MICHAEL'S CHURCH
10 THE OLD SCHOOL
11 THE NORMAN KNIGHT
12 ROSELLA COTTAGE AND WESTCOTE COTTAGE

13 MELBOURNE HOUSE, THE COTTAGE AND FERNDALE COTTAGE
14 OLD POST OFFICE AND TERRACE
15 FOUNTAIN COTTAGE
16 THE FOUNTAIN
17 HARVEY'S FARM BUILDINGS AND LEASOW FARM
18 HILLFOOT COTTAGES

N

TO LONG COMPTON

TO ASCOTT

ASCOTT CORNER

ST MICHAEL'S CHURCH

THE GREEN

FOOT PATH

CASTLE 1

NOT TO SCALE

Ascott

A scott is clearly separated from Whichford by open countryside. The approach to this hamlet is signalled by a line of lime trees [fig 19] on one side, and oaks and ash on the other, forming an avenue. This provides a formal prelude to Ascott, which displays a more rural charm than can be found in Whichford. From the crossroads lies a rare group of handsome houses whose garden lands and wide verges are now part of the landscape. Many are set well back from the road, or are situated down side turnings, thus augmenting Ascott's picturesque and secretive character. The road through the village suddenly closes and becomes not much more than a country lane, enveloped again by a tunnel of trees. This relaxed quality is fragile and any intervention could upset the fine balance between the man-made and the natural.

Until quite recently Ascott consisted of many family-owned small farms. Today the landscape of Ascott is made up of small pastures and old orchards, within which sit more sophisticated dwellings. This character must not be lost.

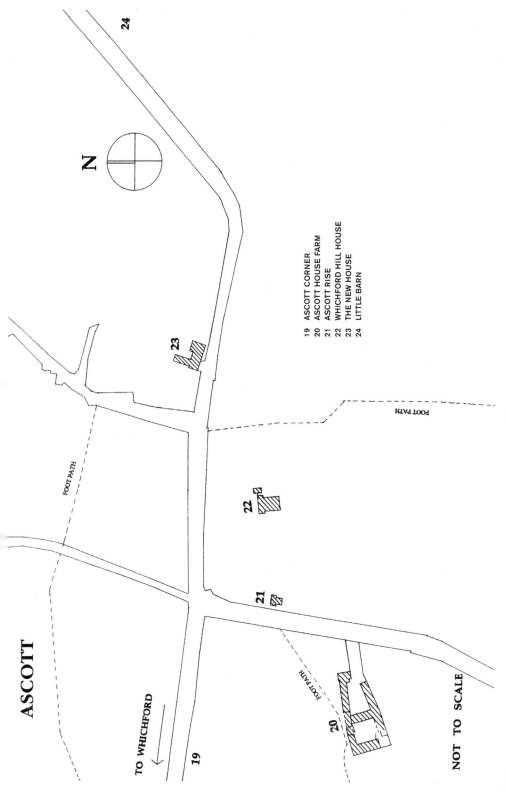

ASCOTT

N

TO WHICHFORD

FOOT PATH

FOOT PATH

FOOT PATH

19   ASCOTT CORNER
20   ASCOTT HOUSE FARM
21   ASCOTT RISE
22   WHICHFORD HILL HOUSE
23   THE NEW HOUSE
24   LITTLE BARN

19
20
21
22
23
24

NOT TO SCALE

ARCHITECTURAL FEATURES: PICTORIAL GUIDE

I t is not possible to list all the buildings that make up the Parish of
Whichford, but recorded here are those buildings which give these
villages their special character.

Our eyes will tell us about the real history of the village and of how
subtly these buildings have responded to social and economic change
over the centuries. Our aesthetic enjoyment will in part be dependant on
reading these changes, and in perceiving how craftsmen have
transformed mere utility into something we find pleasing.

The Green

1 THE CASTLE

The Norman de Mohuns built a castle commanding the valley and their demesne. This was likely to have been a grand house rather than a fortified castle. It was only later in the 13th century, when John de Mohun acquired additional lands at Long Compton that the curtain wall and moat were added. Long Compton was on the route from important centres in the Midlands to the former capital of England at Winchester, and the elevated position of Whichford was a natural location for defending the de Mohuns' lands.

Nothing remains today of the castle above ground, although the foundations are quite extensive. The stones we see today bear little reality to the original castle; only the picturesque moat remains as a reminder of Norman Whichford.

The virid waters of the moat placidly reflect the even greener leaves of the surrounding poplars and recall something of Northern France. This is one of the secret delights of Whichford.

2 THE OLD RECTORY

The visitor arriving from Long Compton is greeted by two buildings that act as an entrance to Whichford. The first is curiously named The Old Rectory, formerly known as Lower End Farm. Today it provides a form of street theatre, whereby girls in jodhpurs and jeans busy themselves with bridles, bits and horseboxes. The present appearance of this house, with two front doors either side of a central staircase, belies a much older house behind the more recent additions to the road frontage. A feature of interest is one of the several village fountains set into the wall at the crossroads.

3   BARRETT'S HILL

A delightful pair of semi-detached cottages set high on the bank. This is an example of the 19th century estate cottage, beautifully detailed with a full understanding of the grammar and use of stone. Openings are dressed in cut stone and celebrate their function, be it a window opening with its dripstone lintel or a corner quoin. A stone string-course binds the two semi-detached dwellings and helps to reduce their apparent size. The front doors are given their appropriate importance by being recessed. While this is essentially a two-storey building, its scale is reduced by low eaves and generous, but well proportioned, dormers. This is a model of a vernacular style well interpreted by its architect.

4 POTTERY HOUSE

The garden here is a splendid overture to the village. Its tilting topiary stand like intoxicated chess pieces out of Lewis Caroll. This is the epitome of the cottage garden design, where artlessness conceals considerable care and imagination. Although the house is modest, its vernacular extension and outbuildings accommodate many craftsmen and their kilns for this world-famous pottery. The most recent building is a clay-tiled Octagon exhibiting the work of selected craftsmen. Architecturally, the lesson that can be learned from this is that it is possible to provide rural industry without suffering visual intrusion.

5   KING EDWARD TERRACE

King Edward Terrace is an important feature within the townscape of Whichford. Architecturally, its interest may lie in detecting the changes that it has undergone over the years. The first storey has clearly been raised as can be seen from the stonework; massive brick chimneys with Tudoresque details have been constructed, and the roof slates have been laid longitudinally. Forming part of King Edward Terrace is Plum Tree Cottage, with its charming feature of decorated entrance from the road. In this case, the garden gate and fence provide a pleasing structure for the abundance of plant material. The garden within becomes a private and protected place.

6 WOOD FARM HOUSE

Standing back from the street, with its neat railed front garden, we find a model of modest good manners. This is a three-bay, well-made symmetrical fronted house with a central portico; the corners and window openings are quoined with stopped chamfered lintels over and a string-course at first floor. The metal windows would appear to be original. All this adds to a delightful sense of repose and ease. Here is an object lesson in the use of local materials and traditional construction. If this lesson is well learned we have a design tool for the future.

7 THATCHED COTTAGE

O pposite Wood Farm House is Thatched Cottage. This cottage is indicative of the small cottages that must have clustered around the church before the 19th century developments introduced by the Weston Park Estate. Stone slates were always expensive and difficult to transport, and reeds for thatch were the most common rural form of roofing material in this area before the 19th century. Welsh slate gradually became available with the opening up of the canals. The advantage of Welsh slate over Stonesfield slate or thatch was that a lower pitch of roof was possible, and this made for a certain economy of construction. It is possible today in Whichford to trace roofing alterations made in response to these changes of fashion and building construction.

A further example of thatch can be seen at the Old House, adjacent to the church. Thatch in Whichford would traditionally have been of reeds cut from the River Stour. This material demanded a steep pitch, with deep overhanging eaves to shed the elements. Beneath a thatched roof the rooms were small, and if they were to be adequately lit the windows had to be set high in the roof, with the thatch wrapped around the openings, like a comfortable duvet. The windows of Thatched Cottage have been restored to their correct size and proportion. The thatched roof provides a delight to the eye as we enjoy the thatcher's skill and his sense of play, which transforms mere utility into a thing of beauty: the essence of architecture.

8 WHICHFORD HOUSE

Whichford House, formerly the vicarage, is by far the most important domestic building in Whichford. It must now rank among the very best houses in Warwickshire, having been beautifully restored (*c*.2007). Within the house is a large 17th century core to which an early 18th century frontage was added. Unfortunately, this was not originally completed, and the house remained until very recently asymmetrical and visually unresolved. Today, the fine 18th century façade, now complete, addresses the street in the correct manner, the symmetry being augmented by fine new metal gates, supported by generous ball-capped piers either side. This restoration has made an enormous contribution to the public perception and enjoyment of Whichford.

9 ST MICHAEL'S CHURCH

The most prominent and important building in Whichford is St Michael's Church. The earliest features of the church are Norman, notably the south doorway, which is supported by a fine arch displaying a decorated tympanum. The main feature of the church is its three-storey tower, begun *c*.1300 but showing clear signs of its having been constructed over several periods. This tower rises up out of the valley and can be seen for miles around. Another fine feature of the church are the five very striking perpendicular clerestory windows. A recent design feature worthy of note is the use of old tombstones to form a processional route from the gate to the church door.

10 THE OLD SCHOOL

Two buildings form this group; only the three-storey building the School House is listed, but it is the single-storey building that is most prominent and forms a satisfying backdrop to the Green. We have here a good example of how careful restoration and adaptation may even enhance an original structure. The Old School has considerable character and now has an air of comfortable domesticity. Although this is a low-lying horizontal building, the feeling of verticality in the windows reflects the scale and arrangement of earlier vernacular buildings in Whichford [see fig. 17].

11 THE NORMAN KNIGHT

Today the Norman Knight, the public house, stands somewhat open and exposed. It is an important element in the composition of the village but it has suffered from the development of the plots on either side. Formerly it was known as The New Inn, and had an air of respectable gentility, with its plate-glass sash windows and projecting front bay. Modern metal windows have disturbed this sense of repose. Apart from the Pottery it is the only commercial building in these villages, and it is right that it should appear a little different from its neighbours. It is to be hoped that the publicans will continue their current work of enhancement. Landscaping can contribute to the townscape as effectively as buildings.

12 ROSELLA COTTAGE AND
WESTCOTE COTTAGE

The road to Ascott out of Whichford is lined for twenty-five yards by two rows of vernacular cottages; the first two on the left are stone-faced. They give way to two cottages of local Warwickshire rose-pink brick, where the most interesting feature is the use of what is known as rat-trap bond. This is a method of laying bricks on edge with the large face exposed and alternating with the small header, which ties the front skin of brickwork to an inner skin. This is a rare example of a traditional bond and entertains the eye.

13 MELBOURNE HOUSE, THE COTTAGE AND FERNDALE COTTAGE

The cottages on the opposite side of the road are all of stone. At Melbourne House simple railings, with delicate finials, separate the house from the footpath. These railings signal to the passer-by a pride of possession and imply an impulse for decoration that here is wholly appropriate and charming. In the 19th century this was the house of the blacksmith, an important tradesman. No doubt the railings were a testimony to his skill. The forge was next door. The gable end displays the patterned cavities of a former pigeon loft.

Another interesting stone detail is found on The Cottage. The local red marlstone is laid with slivers of oolitic limestone. This gives a decorative banding appearance. The two types of stone were often found within the same quarry. Apart from being a decorative feature, it would have the practical advantage of making the coursing easier for the mason.

Both The Cottage and its neighbour Ferndale Cottage display traces of their roofs having been raised when roofing materials changed from thatch to their present slate.

14 THE OLD POST OFFICE AND TERRACE

The Old Post Office itself has signs of its more recent alteration; the additional projecting former shop window provides a visual stop to the terrace and helps to turn the corner. These little changes add variety because they are contained within a repertoire of existing forms. The next house has a classical door case that gives this row of vernacular dwellings an air of modest distinction: an example of where a small detail conveys a public benefit well beyond its confines. The remaining cottages to the south have had modern dormers inserted, with flat lintels, and this breaks away from the established vernacular form of their neighbours. Here, as elsewhere, the front garden wall is an important ingredient within the townscape, as it defines the boundary between the public and the private realm.

15 FOUNTAIN COTTAGE

This house has undergone many changes over time. On the gable end
we can see how the roof has been raised. The metal windows on the
ground floor, with stone segmental arches, would indicate a previous
use before its conversion to a home. The lattice porch, while being
functional, introduces a pleasing element of play.

16   THE FOUNTAIN

This is a 19th century construction housing the village pump. It takes
its cue from 18th century grottoes where salvaged materials were
collaged together decoratively. Here, a rustic outer arch is contrasted by
an inner cut-stone arch with keystone, one arch emphasizing the other.
Much of the stonework has been given a decorative finish. The bucolic
reference is continued by the use of a fragment of vermiculated stone
to support the waterspout. In the classical language of architecture the
use of vermiculation (or worm casts in stone) was seen as a metaphor
for the country.

17 HARVEY'S FARM BUILDINGS AND LEASOW FARM

This is an impressive range of farm buildings around an enclosed yard. Economic changes in agriculture will doubtless produce pressure to develop buildings such as these, and every effort must be made to retain their essential architectural quality. This quality consists of simple strength derived from the size and scale of the building. The scale is enhanced by the punched holes that form deep ground-floor windows, contrasted with the large barn openings carried on shallow cut-stone arches. The roofline is unadorned.

Leasow Farm is a fine 16th-century Cotswold village house that admirably demonstrates the grammar of stone construction. Take for example the windows: on the ground floor are windows of four lights with slim mullions; centrally positioned above them are windows with three lights, and above those are attic windows in the gables with two lights. This arrangement, storey by storey, of slim mullions with short-spanned window heads one above the other is a perfect example of the use of stone as a load-bearing material. We read the correctness not only with our eyes but feel it almost physically, and this may be a source of our pleasure.

18 HILLFOOT COTTAGES

Here is a cleverly designed pair of cottages resembling a single house or lodge to a country estate. A considerable amount of three-dimensional play has been permitted without losing the essential simplicity of a stone building. Windows are still vertically proportioned, slate gives way to decorative clay roof tiles, and the eaves and bargeboards overhang to give shelter and protection to the stone walls below.

19 ASCOTT CORNER

The small pumping station on the road to Ascott provides something of the *Shock of the New*.[3] Being smaller than a house, it has a slightly surreal presence in the landscape. Its isolation, solitude and scale remind us of a painting by Magritte, who famously named a picture of a pipe as *This is not a Pipe*. We might label this little construction 'This is not a House'. A certain poetry can be derived from its incongruity, which would immediately vanish if another building were to be placed beside it.

This road leads us, via a line of limes and oak trees, to the crossroads at Ascott Hill.

20 ASCOTT HOUSE FARM

The soft rolling landscape between Ascott and Whichford has been augmented by fine tree planting at Ascott House Farm. Here the traditional principles of good husbandry have been employed: specimen trees will provide shelter for the animals; pride in these trees is emphasized by the robust tree guards that have been installed.

Across the field the arcaded forms of the former cart hovels of the Victorian Ascott House Farm present an almost Italianate appearance: *Ascott in Chianti*.

21   ASCOTT RISE

Another house almost certainly built as a lodge lies at the foot of Ascott Hill. The interest here is in the deliberate use of Victorian picturesque details to emphasise its bucolic setting. These details include decorative overhanging bargeboards and emphatic quoining to the corners and around the window openings. The lattice porch is a gesture to the public nature of architecture which we all enjoy. Undoubtedly these features owe much to that prolific writer on gardens, John Claudius Loudon. His *Encyclopedia of Cottage, Farm and Villa Architecture and Furniture* (1833)[4] was very influential. He, himself, was active at Ditchley Park, and nearby for General Stratton at Great Tew, where he set up a school for the theory of farming earlier in the century.

The eye is caught at the crossroads by the avenue of chestnuts and other fine trees leading to pretty Combe House.

22 WHICHFORD HILL HOUSE

Originally Whichford Hill House was a small farmhouse, that was extended at the time of the Whichford Parish Enclosures Act, 1805. This is a simple, if not austere, classical 3-bay house. It has a number of features, such as string-courses and mannerist projecting keystones, which more properly would belong to a building of an earlier period. Its ashlar stone is not local, and the use of this more expensive stone indicates an attempt to aggrandise a former farmhouse.

49

23 THE NEW HOUSE

This is a building of considerable interest in its eclectic collection of architectural details. This substantial Victorian house is now joined to an earlier cottage, the most prominent feature of which is a projecting stone and slated oven, a local feature found in 17th century buildings. The neo-Greek acanthus-topped railings are a surprising element. Less surprising, but impressive, are the large chimney stacks set on the diagonal.

Here is a very successful barn conversion. The scale and simplicity of the original has been carefully retained. This conversion clearly demonstrates that with care the visual strength of the original building need not be lost by its being adapted for modern use. It also demonstrates that simple buildings have the power to move us as much as something more complex.

THE SECRET LIFE OF THE PLACE

No true understanding of Whichford and Ascott can be gained without experiencing its secret life. A cat's cradle of pathways and bridleways links the secret places of these two villages, and joins them to the surrounding hills. Exploring these footways, one has a glimpse of more ancient settlements stretching back to Saxon times and before. This gentle network of field paths is echoed by little passageways within the villages, all overgrown with Honeysuckle and Queen Anne's Lace, Coltsfoot and Columbine: a secret Arden that we have a duty to nurture, to hold in trust, and to bequeath.

ARCHITECTURAL SYNTAX

Architectural syntax derives in large measure from the correct use of materials. The building materials in these parts are either stone or brick. These two materials have distinct properties and our pleasure in experiencing them lies in recognizing how their essential character has been respected. Stone is quarried from the earth and has to be cut into blocks. It has a very high compressive strength but little tensile strength: that means that it cannot be used to span wide openings. In order to span wide openings an arch has to be formed, therefore blocks of stone or brick are used in compression.

Brick is also a compressive material with no tensile strength, therefore openings in a brick face have to be carried by either a simple timber lintel or by an arch made up of individual bricks cut and shaped to form a series of wedges. Sometimes an arch permits individual uncut bricks to be laid to form a simple arch. By concentrating on essential details such as the window openings and the arch over or on the window cills below, the designer has considerable freedom of expression.

The roof and its bargeboards is another source for decoration. The chimney is an important element in domestic architecture. It punctuates the skyline and denotes the individual house; symbolically it represents the idea of hearth and home. Unfortunately, stone is not the ideal material for chimneys, as the sulphur from the fire can combine with the rain to form a mild acid, which erodes the stone. Therefore many chimneys are either lined with brick or are constructed out of brick.

The pitch of the roof is another important feature. When used correctly this conveys a sense of repose. Stone slates are heavy and are laid in diminishing sizes at a steeper pitch than Welsh slates. Cotswold slates should be laid at a pitch of around 51 degrees. Welsh slate can be laid at a lower pitch, down to 30 degrees or less, although this may give a weaker appearance, and should be avoided in a predominantly Cotswold area. Our pleasure in architecture is often dependent on scale and materials.

Scale and materials

Scale is distinct from mere size; scale in design is essentially the relationship of one part to another, and in building, scale is dependent on those parts being related to the proportions of man. This ratio, and how it is used in architecture, is often affected by the choice of materials. A brick building, for instance, will often have a repetition of smaller elements, forming larger wholes.

Often deliberate changes of scale are used to give expression. A good example of this deliberate use of large scale details to emphasize a particular building or its role, is to be seen in the little lodge building known as Ascott Rise. Here large deep lintels with their pronounced projecting keystones, the quoining around the window openings and at the corners, together with emphatic decorated bargeboards, are deliberately used to symbolise ideas of the country.

Scale is not just confined to the designing of a single building but must extend into how buildings are grouped, and even to the space between buildings. Too small a structure can be as conspicuous and discordant as one that is too large. One way of ensuring compatible scale is to confine oneself to the correct use of materials found locally, as this is likely to ensure a consistent repertoire of forms.

Brick and stone are load-bearing materials and give rise to the vertical proportions which we find in these traditional buildings. It is something of a solecism to introduce horizontal forms and upset the established pattern for a limestone area. This applies to single-storey buildings no less than to strip or picture windows.

Barns and their conversion present a particular problem in the retention of their original sense of scale. A good example of a successful conversion can be found at Little Barn in Ascott. The original design and scale has been kept by retaining the traditional features of barn door and blank walls facing the road. The strong verticality and drama of the doors has not been weakened by introducing glazing or modern materials.

Scale must also extend into those other elements of the townscape such as roads, footpaths, street furniture and signage.

Materials

Traditionally, Whichford and Ascott were built of the local Marlstone. In more important buildings architectural details were formed out of oolite freestone, also found locally. The oolite was easier to cut and shape. Brick was also used extensively, these two villages being on the edge of the Cotswold escarpment, where stone beds give way to more general clay.

Stonesfield slates, the Cotswold stone roofing slate, had to travel some distance; therefore, its use in areas such as Whichford was relatively rare and would be confined to the more important buildings. Generally, ordinary buildings would have been covered in thatch of reed found locally in the River Stour. This eventually gave way to a more general use of Welsh slate, which could be transported by canal and later by rail.

In this area where stone is still quarried and where the trade of the stonemason is widely practised, every effort should be made to retain this material for building. Reconstituted stone should be avoided, as it gives a mechanical appearance and weathers poorly. Blue slate is also easily obtained and should be used in preference to artificial slate. However, excellent hand-made reproduction Cotswold roofing slates are available and can be used in certain positions.

Brick is also to be seen in these two villages and it can be considered a local material. Great care must be made, however, in selecting a good brick, as bricks are no longer made locally. Hand-made bricks are readily available and these should be laid using a traditional bond, such as Flemish bond. The pleasure we get from brickwork derives from the warmth and colour of the brick and the liveliness of traditional bonds. In Whichford and Ascott brick has generally been confined to dressings.

One of the most important ingredients affecting the appearance of the building is the choice of mortar. When using stone, it is important that the mortar is not too strong and does not contain too much cement. Stone absorbs water, and this water should be allowed to evaporate through the joints. A strong cement mortar will prevent evaporation, and the water will have no alternative but to dry out through the face of the stone: this action, particularly in periods of frost, will eventually erode the face of the stonework. A weak mortar should always be used with stone, and an ideal mix for the locally found rubble stonework is a mix of 7 parts sand to 1 part of cement. The best sand is a mixture of sharp, coarse and building sand. Some builders' merchants will have this already mixed in the right proportions.

Although Ashlar cut stone is not used extensively in these villages, where it is used the mortar joints should be fine and inconspicuous. To assist this, a mortar mix of silver sand, stone dust and lime should be used. Should a dusting of cement be required then white cement should be used.

Windows

Windows are an important feature of any building, their openings should express the load-bearing nature of stone and brick. Traditionally in Whichford and Ascott, windows are vertical in proportion, or made up of vertical parts. All new windows, rather than replacement windows, are today required to be double-glazed against heat-loss. Well-proportioned, double-glazed windows may be difficult to obtain from a catalogue, but purpose-made windows need not be expensive, good local joiners can provide elegant windows with slim glazing bars that meet the building regulations. Some 19th century buildings used metal-framed windows. These windows are still made and are designed to meet the new building regulations.

Local Suppliers

Some of the best artificial slates are produced locally and can be obtained from:

Cardinal Cast Slates Ltd,
Claywell Farm, Aston Road,
Near Ducklington, Witney,
Oxfordshire OX29 7QZ
T: 01993 778 557

A good local source of ready-mixed sand is:

Hickman Bros Landscapes Ltd,
Shipton Hill,
Fulbrook, Burford,
Oxfordshire OX18 4BZ
T: 01993 822 226
F: 01993 823 666

For windows two local firms are:

The Cotswold Casement Company,
Cotswold Business Village, London Road,
Moreton-in-Marsh,
Gloucestershire GL56 0JQ
T: 01608 650 568
F: 01608 651 699
www.cotswold-casements.co.uk

Holdsworth Windows Ltd,
Darlingscote Road,
Shipston Industrial Estate,
Shipston-on-Stour,
Warwickshire CV36 4PR
T: 01608 661 883
F: 01608 661 008
www.holdsworthwindows.co.uk

AFTERWORD – POSTSCRIPT AND PROMISE

A lthough the Parish Plans prepared by the Parishes themselves will not become statutory documents, it is to be hoped that they will help to open up an additional dialogue with the planners. The involvement of local communities in drawing up plans for their own areas will inevitably provide a different emphasis and possible shift of focus in forming planning judgments. At their best the Parishes ought to be able to bring to the debate a more finely tuned and sensitive understanding of their own particular areas.

The ownership of property and the right to develop it, at least from the time of John Locke in the 17th century, has always been held to be a bastion of civil liberty. Rightly therefore our planning laws have had a presumption in favour of development. Given this presumption in planning law, it is hardly surprising that hard pressed planning authorities when faced with what might appear to be a minor application will at times lower their critical sights, rather than run the risk of a lengthy and expensive planning appeal. One of the purposes of this book is to demonstrate that all development, however small, in rural areas such as ours is significant.

Planning is essentially concerned with the competition between the individual and the community for limited resources: between the freedom of the individual and the public good. However because architecture and building comprise a public art, which we are all obliged to share, there can in fact be little development that is strictly private. This is even more so in areas like Whichford and Ascott where the surrounding landscape is paramount, and the balance between built form and landscape is delicate and even fragile.

Aristotle warned that we are all more careful of our own possessions than of those owned communally, and that we are always more inclined to neglect to care for that which is held communally.[5] This tension between the individual interest and what might be regarded as the common good, is often referred to in planning theory as the *'Tragedy of the Commons'*. Originally this was about the dilemma faced by local communities before the Enclosures in preventing the overgrazing of common land. Today there are similar planning problems of a social nature, as we face the prospect of global warming. Simply put, we may all know the direct cost to us as individuals of reducing our carbon footprint, but how do we weigh this known cost against the unknown costs and benefits at a later date? – benefits that will accrue not just to ourselves, but to others also. What should be our attitude towards those who free ride on our sacrifice and effort? These are the problems, which we will all have to confront in the future and which are bound to become more urgent.

The village forum may well be the best vehicle for addressing these issues. As we share so much in common, it could be that the aesthetic values which we seek to uphold and for which we have been invited to take additional responsibility, will stiffen the necessary moral values with which to approach a difficult future.

In which case Edmund Burke's little platoon can march forward in greater confidence. Burke's expression of the ideals of community has never been bettered:

'To be attached to the subdivision, to love the little platoon we belong to in society, is the first principle (the germ as it were) of public affections. It is the first link in the series by which we proceed toward a love of our country and to mankind. The interest of that portion of social arrangement is a trust in the hands of all those who compose it; and as none but bad men would justify it in abuse, none but traitors would barter it away for their own personal advantage.'[6]

PLANNING POLICIES AFFECTING WHICHFORD AND ASCOTT

Both Whichford and Ascott are designated in the Local Plan as being within the **Cotswolds Area of Outstanding Natural Beauty**. This gives the Planners considerable powers to control development that might damage or pose a threat to this special area.

Small individual developments, which might in themselves be modest, can cumulatively change an area. Unless development is controlled and undertaken with considerable care the change may be for the worse. Paradoxically it is because these two villages are architecturally modest and the balance between built form and the landscape is so delicate that any ill-considered development can have a disproportionate impact.

Fortunately in the **Stratford-on-Avon District Local Plan Review 1996–2011** the Council set out clear policies for protecting and enhancing environmental features. **Section 4.2** deals with the **Cotswold Area of Outstanding Natural Beauty**, under their **Policy EF.1** – to quote:

> The special qualities of those parts of the Cotswold Area of Outstanding Natural Beauty which lie within Stratford-on-Avon District, as defined on the Proposals Map, will be protected and where opportunities arise, be enhanced. Development proposals should be founded on a high degree of sensitivity towards the natural beauty of the landscape and towards the special qualities and features that contribute to the distinctive character of the area. Proposals which would have a detrimental impact on the AONB will not be permitted, whether located within the AONB or outside the designated area.
>
> Assessment of proposals will also take into account the potential cumulative impact of development, particularly in relation to the rural tranquillity of the area.

In the Council's **Explanation 4.2.2** they go on to add:-

> AONB designation does not rule out all forms of development but the District Planning Authority is not prepared to permit schemes which would be detrimental to the character of the area. It is for architects and designers to put forward proposals which reflect an appreciation of, and sympathy for the special character of the area.

In **Section 5** of the **Local Development Plan Review** the Council set out their policies for promoting and securing appropriate standards of development. This includes layout and design, materials and forms of development within the scheme, and landscaping etc. The Planners therefore have wide powers in place to insist on a high standard of design in areas such as Whichford and Ascott. It is to be hoped that this book will encourage a real partnership between the planners and the people of these two villages to bring about a more vigorous and satisfactory control of development.

NOTES

1 Burke, Edmund, *A Philosophical Enquiry into the Origin of our Ideas of the Sublime and Beautiful*, ed James T Boulton, Basil Blackwell, 1987.
2 Tradition has it that, in the early years of the Civil War, a local man, uncertain of his loyalty, agreed to betray the Royalist Army. He is supposed to have stood on the packhorse bridge beside the ford and dropped a stone over the side to indicate in which direction the Royalists had gone.
3 Hughes, Robert, *The Shock of the New*, A Knopf, New York, 1981. Published in England following a much acclaimed television series. Robert Hughes dealt with the development of modern art, which was very much concerned with subverting normal perception.
4 Loudon, John Claudius, *An Encyclopedia of Cottage, Farm and Villa Architecture and Furniture*, Henry G. Bohn, London, 1833.
5 *The Politics of Aristotle*, Book 2, Chapter 3, Translated by B. Jowett. First published Oxford University Press, 1905.
6 Burke, Edmund, *Reflections on the Revolution in France*, Penguin ed p 135.

GLOSSARY OF ARCHITECTURAL TERMS

Arch. The spanning of an opening by a form made of several units. In stone or brick these units are often wedge-shaped and are known as voussoirs.

Ashlar. Regular cut stone blocks having a smooth face.

Bargeboard. A timber board fixed on the gable end of a roof to hide the ends of the roof timbers. This is often decorated.

Bond. The laying of bricks in a pattern to ensure strength in a wall. There are many types of bond eg English bond or Flemish bond.

Cill. The bottom member of a window or door opening.

Clerestory. The upper storey with its own line of windows.

Dressing. Decorative patterning around door or window openings and other key features. In Whichford these dressings are usually of brick.

Dripstone. A projecting moulding, to deflect water over a door or window opening.

Keystone. The central unit of an arch.

Lintel. A single member spanning an opening.

Marlstone. A limestone containing clay and iron giving it a brown appearance.

Oolite. A fine-grain limestone that has the appearance of fish eggs, easy to carve.

Perpendicular. A style of late English Gothic architecture, with strong emphasis on the vertical, particularly in the upper tracery of the principal windows.

Quoin. Patterning at the corners of a building or opening. These usually alternate between large and small. Originally quoining was a metaphor for strengthening critical parts.

Townscape. The collective appearance of buildings which form an area, together with its roads, footpaths, planting and street furniture.

Tympanum. The area between a door-head and the arch over, often a place for decoration.

BIBLIOGRAPHY

Beresford, Eric, *St. Michael's Church Whichford: A Brief Guide*, 2005.
A concise guide to the church from Norman times to the present day.

Beresford, Eric, *Whichford: Some Historical Notes Together With Illustrations*, produced on CD-ROM, 2005.
Over fifty illustrations accompany a well researched text.

Hines, William, *Club Day and Carriageway: A Whichford History,* published privately, mid-20th century.
A useful snapshot of Whichford's past.

Maxwell Lyte, H., *A History of Dunster and of the Families of Mohun & Luttrell*, 1909.
Dunster is, of course, in Somerset; it was the other seat of the Norman de Mohuns, who held Whichford after the Conquest.

Pevsner, Nikolaus and Alexandra Wedgwood, *The Buildings of England: Warwickshire*, Penguin Books, 1966.
A standard work of architectural reference, rather thin and disappointing on Whichford.

Warriner, Michael, *A Prospect of Weston*, Roundwood Press (Kineton), 1978.
The Weston Park Estate has been the single most important influence on these villages.

Wood-Jones, Raymond B., *Traditional Domestic Architecture in the Banbury Region*, republished by Wykham Books, 1986.
A comprehensive and scholarly guide to the domestic architecture in the region.

PHILOSOPHY

Architecture is as much an art as a profession, but it is an art in an unusual sense. Absolutely everyone experiences his surroundings, whether or not he has intended this involvement. Architecture and Town Planning are social, public activities, and they are fed by ideas. There is much pleasure to be taken from appreciating these ideas in the buildings around us, and we should recognise the ways in which inevitably buildings and town planning shape our communities and our lives.

Three books have helped this commentary; they offer a way forward in understanding rural communities such as ours.

Burke, Edmund, *Reflections on the Revolution in France*, Penguin Books, 1968. Published by Penguin Classics.
This is the most famous defence of the proposition that society is held together by memory, tradition and its institutions, which are fragile but perforce have to evolve and change in order to survive. This book should be required reading for all architects and town planners.

MacIntyre, Alasdair, *After Virtue: A Study in Moral Theory, Duckworth, 1985.*
This book by an important modern philosopher offers ideas that challenge the conventional assumptions about modernity. It suggests the idea of 'the authority of tradition' in support of the concept of social practice.

Scruton, Roger, *The Aesthetics of Architecture*, Methuen, 1979.
This is the best introduction to the subject of aesthetics in architecture. It underlines the importance of architecture in our daily life. I would also like to reccommend Roger Scruton's *England: an Elegy*, Chatto and Windus, 2000 and *News from Somewhere*, Continumn, 2004, which are among the finest pastoral writings in modern English letters.

BIOGRAPHICAL DETAILS

J OHN MELVIN is an architect and town planner. He trained at the
Architectural Association School of Architecture and at the
Department of Town Planning, University College London. He has won
many awards for his architecture. In 1996 he held the Sargant Fellowship
at the British School at Rome. For many years, he sat on the Bishop of
London's Diocesan Advisory Committee for the Care of Churches. He is
Chairman of the Fabric Advisory Committee of Guildford Cathedral.
John Melvin is married with two children, and lives and works in Ascott.

Part of the Macmillan way which runs through Ascott. This is one of the longest public
footpaths in the country and follows the course of an oolite limestone belt.